Poetic Tails

The Mystical Connection of Horse and Rider

Poetic Tails

The Mystical Connection of Horse and Rider

Marc C. Ness

An Equine Press book

ISBN: 0692523545
ISBN 13: 978-0692523544

Dedication

To my father, his love of literature inspired this book.

And to Graziella-cut your reins free.

Contents

Introduction...viii

The Struggle 2

Discipline 5

A Different Kind of Control 7

Running to Apples..9

Become the Saddle..11

Cushions 13

No Place to Hide 15

Bow Down 17

Change Moves Over...19

This Circular Maze 21

Leave the Arena 23

Ride Without Memory 25

Loose the Rest..27

Ride the Center 29

The Bridle Maker's Knife 31

Equine Religion..33

Cleverness..35

Lift the Saddle 37

Ride the Roses 39

The Farrier's Fire 41

The Master's Craft 43

No Guilt 45

The Joy 48

   Nothing Here 51

   The Hitching Post 53

   A Sound Horse 55

   Thunder Rises 57

   The Spark of Silence..59

   Silken Thread 61

   We Have a Secret..63

   Where Reins Break New Ground 65

   The Heart of the Matter...67

   Leave Behind 69

   Sweet Talk...71

   My Horse 73

   No Pedigree 75

   Learning to Ride..77

   The Color of Gold 79

   Sweeping Whispers...81

   The Equestrian Soul 83

   Ride the Joy 85

   Heart to Heart 87

   The Heart of a Thousand Horses.............................89

   Synonyms 91

   Comfort. 93

Introduction

This book is about horses, but, more importantly, it's about relationships with horses. Relationships come in all forms; we have relationships with our families, our friends, animals, and the universe. Our relationships form our lives; they provide for us an arena of growth in which we transform ourselves in struggle and joy. They help us distinguish real from relative values and reveal the weakness and strength in our hearts. Our views of the world form relationships that whisper clues about the inner mysteries of the universe.

As a poet and a writer, I find that my deepest interest rests in the miraculous connected nature of the universe. The equestrian world is filled with mysterious tales of courage and hope, strength and achievement. It has given me the perfect medium through which to express my writings. I have used my own and others' heartfelt impressions to guide me through this journey. Sometimes they are quick and witty, other times deeply introspective. I have combined short stories with poems to expand the reader's view of his or her own everyday equestrian experience. My intention is to increase the impact of my poetry, not limit the impressions of any experience.

At the center of every relationship is love, that mysterious longing for union. Equestrians love their horses. Their journeys are constant searches for deeper connections to their horses. Inside the heart of every rider is a secret yearning to reach the furthest potentials of horse and human interaction. Like all relationships, that interaction is a mystery—it can't be thought out; it must be experienced. There's a difference between reading about horses and getting on one. We need both, but the latter will give us more understanding than any book could ever teach. Through experience and knowledge we can change our lives and expand our hearts into the greater realms of the universe. This book is a poetic attempt to expand your heart to greater equestrian joy.

Part One

The Struggle

Struggle and joy are interrelated. We need struggle; it is vital to our growth. Struggle is the effort to resolve the tension between the current state of our personal limitations and the hoped-for condition of a higher result. The struggle we endure is the suffering we experience through the sacrifice of individual weaknesses toward the attainment of joy.

Pain is associated to struggle; it is a reactionary response to the personality's ignorance of its present condition. When the ignorance is accepted, pain is transformed, and the struggle becomes a joy. Through the trials of personal experience, compassion aids our struggles by expanding our hearts into the mysterious realms of the universe.

Compassion allows the pain and suffering of human experience. It transforms the pain of existence by accepting obstacles along the way. As we struggle to reduce the tension between horses and ourselves, the more compassion we generate, the more understanding we will gain.

L isten to the story of the saddle being cut into existence. "Once I was alive, giving shelter to those who carried my skin. Then night came, and bones fell to the earth. Sleeping—I lay sleeping."

"Magic hands folded my cells and brought suppleness back again. I wondered what I might become. Pain entered and shaped my soul; crying came at the tip of a knife. Anyone cut has a heart. Now the uncomfortable ride of my seat makes thick skin supple again."

I t was hot that afternoon, and I was tired of holding the saddle. We had attempted this before without any resolution, and I was beginning to question her knowledge. We were trying to break our young colt, but he wanted nothing to do with a saddle. I jokingly said, "Let's buckle that saddle down and go to the rodeo." She looked at me and laughed with a somewhat condescending tone.

She had been telling me over the past few weeks that he wasn't ready, and I was beginning to believe her. The continuous attempts to try to build his trust weren't showing any results. I was frustrated and felt an urge to manhandle the little guy and get on with it, but she insisted otherwise.

I stood there patiently waiting for something to change. She stared into his eyes as if to ask him a question and then said, "He's ready." I gently placed the saddle on his back, and, to my astonishment, he didn't move a muscle. I secured the saddle and all the tack in the usual way while she watched attentively.

I was cautious as I helped her up and over the saddle. She stroked his neck with reassurance and said, "It's OK." His ears, previously facing back, fell forward. He turned his head as his eyes softened and gave a look of acceptance. As she shifted her weight forward, he began walking around the arena with hardly a care in the world.

Discipline

The point is not to break your horse,
anything that is broken is useless.

The lead rope with no buckle
will not give a direction.

Too much authority creates bitterness,
not enthusiasm.

A stallion rules the heard only as long
as they want him to.

The point is to create a relationship,
a useful living thing. A mutual need
based on freedom.

Foster that connection,
then discipline becomes desired.

I watched the elderly woman lead her horse down the barn aisle and into the stall. The lead rope was hanging low down the side of the neck and back up to the owner's hand. There wasn't the usual tension you see in the inexperienced horseman. There was a communication between the two of them that was clear.

They had walked the entire distance from the outside arena back to the barn and into the stall, a distance of some one hundred yards or more. There was nothing unusual about what had occurred until I saw her pull the lead rope with a soft tug off the horse's neck and wind it up into her hand. The rope was never snapped onto the halter; it was only hanging over the neck. The horse had followed her the entire distance without control and walked into its stall.

There is a balance between discipline and control. Discover your own sense of discipline; give yourself the freedom you need, and follow your heart home.

A Different Kind of Control

The bridle is meant to lead, not control.
The wedding ring suggests a union, not a circular cage.

You can own a saddle but not the fit of a horse. That
comes with experience, a different kind of possession.

Short reins leave no choice, like freedom at the end of a
rope. Long reins give no direction, never finding home.

Dinner comes with hay and water,
without the right mixture, cramps.

Sitting in the saddle will not produce a master.
The child wearing a crown cannot manage a kingdom.

One buckle of the crosstie pulls to one side,
both snapped securely create a resting place.

Ride the center between tension and release,
where discipline follows the equestrian heart home.

D o something you enjoy, and observe your reactions. Your physical state will lighten, and your mind will focus naturally with effortless discipline. Your sense of time will drift to the background, giving you a feeling of freedom and detachment from the world. You become absorbed in your own joyful intoxication of the moment.

Now do something you dislike, and observe your reactions. You become agitated, your mind wanders, and you feel tension in your body. There is a slowing of time with a desire to escape the activity. Negative emotions fill your being, and it becomes increasingly difficult to stay in the moment.

The differences in the psychological impact are striking. There are lessons to be learned from experiencing both types of activities, but sometimes the best way to learn something is to do it in an environment of joy. We usually learn more quickly and retain a greater understanding after a joyful experience than a negative one.

Try not to ride for quick control; that is the tempo of fear. Learn from the moment, and ride instead to the rhythmic sound of joyful hooves.

Running to Apples

A horse will run from the sound of spurs,
steel on bone.

That is the tempo of fear,
like the sound of a lion tamer's whip.
Its energy short and sharp and then exhausted.

You ride for quick control, not for the rhythmic
sound of joyful hooves. The stable hand knows
the value of a soft brush.

You can't ease your pain by having dominion over
another. Friends enjoy the compliments of sweet
conversation.

Gravity loosens its grip when hooves
run to apple orchards.

S urprisingly, one of our greatest stumbling blocks to change is the wrong notion of what others have done to achieve success. It is easy to look upon the accomplishments of another and assume that person was born with the gifts he or she has. We all have talents that come more easily to us than to others, but we all must work to achieve our goals. Remember that all abilities are earned, not given.

Acknowledge the abilities in others by praising their efforts to improve their skills. Understand that their merit is the result of frustrating effort, not your misconception of something given. In order for growth to take place, there must be an exchange of energy from a lower to a higher state. In order to get, one must give.

If you want to become something more, there is only one way: break down the obstacles in yourself that impede your growth, work toward a greater understanding of your chosen path, and commit to a long road ahead.

If you want to become a better rider, make the effort necessary to grow. Polish the seat of your soul, wear down your imperfections, and become the saddle being ridden.

Become the Saddle

A custom saddle is a thing of beauty.
You can purchase the tack, but not the master's craft.
That exchange is a foreign currency.

A stolen horse can't be ridden in public.
To ride the parade, you must prove possession.

Frustration in the saddle is the currency to make a
purchase. Peace in the saddle, the result of a frustrated
cantor.

Silver polish contains an abrasive,
remove the grime and spurs will shine.

Years of weather open strands of wood.
Sanding makes the barn door smooth.

Breeches polish the rider's seat,
a wearing down of imperfections.

Turn your riding upside down,
become the saddle being ridden.

In life we usually find ourselves wishing for an easier way. We all want a high-paying job with few hours and a relationship with no effort. That is the imaginative dream we sometimes fall into. While it's entertaining to think about, it's hardly realistic.

One afternoon, I was watching a horse clinic run by a professional rider, trying to learn from his experience. He was clearly skilled in his approach and was passing that information on to the participants. I was hoping to gain some new insight into the relationships between horse and rider.

As the lesson went on, one of the girls was clearly having difficulty with her horse. The trainer kept telling her to stay quiet in the saddle. She was moving from side to side without staying in contact with her horse. It was clear to me as a spectator that she was having one of those days.

This continued on for some time until she burst out in frustration, "I just can't communicate with my horse; he's too difficult." To that, the trainer replied, "Translate your intentions through your saddle." In that moment, the lesson became crystal clear.

We've all heard the old adage: "It's not what you say; it's how you say it." It's just as important to learn how to say something as it is to know what to say. There is discipline in that and skill in translation. Pray for difficult lessons, not an easier life.

Cushions

All riders sit on leather,
a cushion against the equine ego.

The student's wish—a softer seat.
The master's way—a medium for translation.

Pray for skill in conversation,
not an easier ride.

In a manner of speaking, riding a horse is like sitting on a mirror; every move is reflected, every blemish seen. There is anxiety in viewing the truth, the idea that we might have to change. Sometimes we pull back and search for an easier way to reach our goal.

Nothing is more tenacious than a personality defending its beliefs. We use perpetual excuses that exhaust our minds and tire our bodies. The shortcuts we invent are a shallow attempt to surpass the effort to change and deny our own reflections.

Real change is the achievement of a struggle to attain mastery over your own weaknesses. It is the lesson learned from the experience of facing your own reflection in the life you live.

Be thankful for the struggle. Fill your presence in the saddle; use the opportunity to see yourself in the equine mirror, and grow from the experience.

No Place to Hide

There is no place to hide,
sitting here in the saddle.

I want to hide from your presence,
but you know my every move.

I try to conjure tricks,
with quick of hand and sleight of hoof.

No audience here, just you staring back
showing me the looking glass.

Too hot for working,
nowhere to go for shade.

Time to let the saddle hit the rack,
rest until tomorrow.

No more lessons. Just you showing me
that shadows and light the same.

T he black stallion is a symbol of great power and strength, and just like all symbols, it has a multitude of meanings. Sometimes the stallion is thought of as a king, the achievement of royalty. At other times, it symbolizes the dark energy in us that needs to be tamed. But don't be fooled; dark energy is the movement of the forces of nature, and nature cannot be controlled. It can only be surrendered to like facing the fury of an oncoming storm.

Darkness is a part of our lives; it serves the purpose of regenerating our inner selves in order to set us along a new path. We must be willing to face our own darkness, give in to the forces of nature, and allow ourselves to be lifted up to a higher place.

Bow Down

Evening falls on the arena,
the black stallion enters again.

The darkest heart needs the most light.

Running unbroken into the falling sun,
I surrender my imperfections.

Bow down to the darkness,
let the sun circle round your wild heart.

With the energy of falling, the sun rises again.

Without fight the stallion bows down,
leaving darkness, following light.

W hen we're attempting to change, sometimes the best thing we can do is break our daily habits. Habits chain us to our personal history by keeping us on the same course of action, preventing us from experiencing any new perceptions or liberating roads.

When we are under the force of habit, we believe there is no way out, that we are destined to a future linked to our past. It is like a dream running over and over as we sleep from which there is no escape.

Habits cause us to lose touch with our essence by forcing us into the lazy continuation of the past. Reality, however, is constantly changing. It is never the same but a continuous moving moment.

When attempting to change how you ride, have the courage to change your routine. Ride into the arena early on a living moment. Experience the joy of your own being, and move to the sound of a changing rhythm.

Change Moves Over

Ride into the arena early,
just when the sun is breaking.

That's when change moves over
sleeping equine hearts.

Be the first one in and the last one out.

Be there inside the outside,
where souls move in the lighted
sound of lifted hooves.

S ometimes personal effort isn't enough; for all we do, there are times when we fall short of our expectations. Again and again, we turn around ourselves, looking for results. We search for answers in the one place we will never find them, in the knotted maze of our minds.

Exhausted from our struggles, we find that there is only one thing left to do—surrender to something higher and wait for equine grace.

This Circular Maze

My heart is tied to the hitching post,
I circle round attempting freedom.

The horse cannot untie itself.

This history has me tired,
like the stable hand at the end of the day.

Sacked out in the prison of my own
circular knotted maze...

I wait for equine grace.

R outine is the rut we lazily fall into that binds us by obligation to forces that we are typically unconscious of. It forces us to repeat our mistakes and creates an attachment to our egotistical selves that separates us from our individual sense of responsibility and deeper nature.

Our deeper nature radiates the individual light of our own joy. It shines through continuously; like the spark of a sharpened spur, it grabs our attention in a gleaming moment. Yet it remains hidden behind the dust of yesterdays past.

To live in the moment is a constant struggle against the rut of routine; to ride in the moment is a difficult task. Both require a sort of double attention, looking both inward and outward at the same time. It is like sitting on the edge of a knife; there is a constant vigilance to remain in perfect balance.

Live your life in the perfect moment. Break the battle of endless turning; cut your girth clean, and ride the light of your own joy.

Leave the Arena

Sometimes the moons dust falls on the arena,
dark shining flakes make soft footing where riders' turn.

Break the battle of endless turning.
Ride where masters ride,
on the edge of the harness maker's knife.

Cut the girth clean.
Ride the spark of a sharpened spur,
the tangent light of the equestrian soul.

Leave the arena,
ride the darkened aisle through the
barn doors into light.

A powerful memory is a useful skill. It provides for us a sense of security, knowing we have at our command the information we need to maneuver effectively in the world. Remembering the signs of a long trail ride will steer us home. A good memory is a function we all admire and value for its importance.

Sometimes, though, without our knowing, memory hinders rather than helps by restricting our choices to those of the past. A memory of a broken heart restricts our courage and keeps us from finding new joys in relationships. And the memory of expectations, if seen in the wrong light, weighs heavily in the moment, causing us to believe that today should be just like yesterday.

Give up the weight of memory and release your negative past. Ride like a leaf in the wind, and become a plaything of the universe.

Ride Without Memory

Sit in the saddle like a leaf in the wind.

Let the great equestrian breath take
your weight away, that courage comes
from the heart.

Freedom releases the grievous past.

Ride without the weight of memory,
where horse and rider are free.

L oss is difficult to absorb. It's the pain of giving up something you hold dear. But it's not just the unexpected losses in life that we have to learn to navigate; it's the small everyday challenges that can be so difficult. To change our minds and lose an idea can be the most challenging thing of all. Whenever we are attempting to learn something new, we struggle between gaining new knowledge and holding on to our past concepts.

Riding a horse in the same old way is both a blessing and a curse. There is a balance between the technique we know and the lesson to be learned. In order to gain a new strength in the saddle, we must keep what is of value and lose the old concepts holding us back.

Our minds are mystical places where thoughts rise of their own accord and new concepts become a thing of beauty. Find the balance between profit and loss; then lose the rest.

Loose the Rest

When reins will of their own accord,
a turn becomes equine beauty.

Listen to all the trainers from history,
their words can never explain that.

Inside the sphere of the four great pillars,
silence is the best instructor.

Imitate the technique of your trainer,
but never rely on that for your balance.

Balance is found between profit and loss.
Pay your trainer the respect she deserves,
then lose the rest.

T he history of a horse's life can be seen in the growth rings around its hoof. Like the rings of a tree, it demonstrates the abundance or lack of proper nutrition from its past. Poor nutrients and continuous stress create scars and uneven rings. Healthy food and a safe environment are observed as uniform growth stemming from the center.

Similar to a horse, our experiences are shown by the joys and scars written on the heart. When we are joyful, our hearts expand; when we are injured, our hearts contract, reducing the joyful influences on the circumferences of our lives.

When an injury occurs, the effects remain; the scarred rings of yesterday are the darkened shadows of our past. But the hoof grows out, and eventually the damaged portion is cut away and discarded. We grow, too, and like the hoof can cut away our past and expand from our center.

The center of the universe is the heart, spinning around itself, radiating the light of joy. The center of your horse is the light of a heart filled ribcage. Release your circular past, and increase the light of your own joy.

Ride the Center

Inside the ring of hooves, let go and die.
The way to ride is in the center.

Reins-stirrups-saddle-horse, become the center.
The center of a star is the light it gives off.

Ride like color bursting across the sunrise.
Find the center of the equestrian universe
spinning light at lights speed.

Yesterday your heart was dark;
shadow on shadow, black on black.

Yesterday's gone...

Escape to the center of a colored ribcage.
Ride in the center of the spinning colored
heart where straw turns to gold.

For centuries, mankind has explained the mysteries of the universe through the use of symbolism, ancient myths, and poetry. The Greeks attempted to explain love through Aphrodite and personify the forces of nature in the winged stallion Pegasus.

Poets use the chaotic nature of the moon's influence to counteract the separation between reality and illusion. The darkening phase of the moon represents destruction with all its ill effects. But darkness seen with the wisdom of light brings the power to heal or transform. When we realize that the moon's light is only a reflection of the sun shining off its surface, we can separate in ourselves the shadows from the light and give the moon a whole new meaning.

When we fight against the moon, we fight against ourselves. Understand the psychological phases of the moon, and release yourself from its pulling metaphorical influence. Sit in the saddle of your true essence, and ride without restraint.

The Bridle Maker's Knife

Sometimes you ride at midnight when the
chaps of the moon fall on the arena.
You forget the moon's clothes and yours
are the same.

Your horse knows the essence, not
the form of your technique. The same
word can have a thousand meanings.

Forceful reins produce only argument.
Think instead of the bridle maker's knife,
and cut your reins free.

W e are a part of the earth, not just symbolically speaking but in reality. Our cells are made of the same elemental substances that the earth is also made of, like water, carbon, and iron.

Iron is an element in our blood; it helps transfer oxygen to our cells. It is also the metaphorical symbol of our sacrifice. It is said that we bleed when we make a tremendous effort or sacrifice to achieve a goal.

In the arena or on the trail, there is a constant interplay between horse and rider that creates a splendid mixture for growth. Sometimes, despite our efforts, we still fall short, and at other times we gain unexpected joys in the strangest ways.

When you view time on your horse as an opportunity to learn then you write a type of story, a kind of personal religion for yourself. That story will write itself as you open up to the lessons that your horse is constantly giving you. Listen to your horse, and it will show you the beauty of all your experiences in the same light, one of growth.

Equine Religion

Your equine religion is written in the arena.
That is where blood stains the earth.

Hard bucks and good luck all the same
light shining.

You send me all the impossible.
I try the straight and narrow,
but nothing moves here.

All I see is the sound of thundering hooves.
All I hear is the flowing mane in the wind.

All the same sight listening.

W hen it comes to cleverness, the mind is a one-way trap—one way in with no way out. The more you believe that you are being clever, the more self-deluded you become. Cleverness is a sharpened display of superficial skill used to gain an advantage.

Awareness, on the other hand, is the recognition of the subtler states of ourselves and our environment. It is a broadening of our experiences, not a narrowing of concentration. These experiences lift the soul and provide for us a lasting feeling of connection to the world.

The next time you ride, try not to outsmart your horse by using misleading, superficial control. That is an illusion of the moment like the shadow and light of the world. Go deeper for what you want; go inside the heart, and ride the constant state of vigilance, where horse and rider find sweetness of the soul.

Cleverness

Riding the equestrian heart
is not a magician's trick.

Shadow and smoke,
no help there.

Don't deceive yourself.

Cleverness is a trick of the mind,
subtle yet sharp.

Superficial skill not as lasting as
sweetness of the soul.

Anyone who has ever been in a relationship knows the importance of the right environment. For the growth of anything, the appropriate conditions must be present. A seed will stay dormant until the proper environmental conditions become available. Bring about the pureness of conditions to which it corresponds, and the proper fruit will appear.

Every relationship we experience, whether horse or human, is caught between the two contradictory poles of the mind and heart, between separation and union. The mind with its grasping tendencies attempts to create harmony by possessing the object of its desire and the realization of its goal. This is the satisfaction of a material possession and not the expression of a true joy. The heart with its tendencies toward expansion listens to the mind without discrimination or violence. When it hears the proper reason to which it corresponds, the seed is opened and the truth revealed.

Create in yourself the right conditions for the experience of truth. Put your mind in service to the heart; form the proper environment in your relationships, and the truth will reveal itself to you.

Lift the Saddle

Every horse has one message.
It says, "I have a heart!"

Die to me and you can ride
the rhythm of a heartbeat.

Lift the saddle and see what's
underneath the blanket.

Tight reins tell me about possession,
that is a grasping shallow life.

The record of my life is written
from my heart. The sum of your life
is measured by your heart.

Our relationship is weighed by where we meet.
Meet me at the arena of misty clouds,
where hooves make no sound.

There...you will see the truth of me.

It seems that we are constantly caught in the alternating forces of the universe. The attempt to maintain a sense of direction continually forces us into a movement of swinging to and fro, back and forth. This is the seesaw energy of the universe, which, if resisted, gives rise in us to the inevitable emotions of hope and despair. Paradoxically, the more we resist, the more under its power we fall and the greater our struggle becomes.

But the struggle cannot be avoided; it must be taken up in the arena of our lives and transformed by the awareness of its direction and the contrary use of its energy. Just as a rider uses the rebound from her saddle to spring upward again and then alternately lets gravity pull her weight into the saddle, a smooth cantor is achieved with the least amount of energy expanded.

Use the alternating forces of horse and rider wisely. Like a smoothly ridden cantor, give the pendulum energy; ride the wave of expansion and contraction, creating a balance of equine motion.

Ride the Roses

Every day you're looking to ride the weather.
Sunshine one day, rain the next.

You carve arcs with hooved blades,
planting seeds of equine beauty.

Storm clouds or sunny skies the same,
a mixture of weathers' union.

Ride the state where thorn and
fragrance form the rose.

In that place gardens are grown.

F arriers use their skill to form metal through heat and pressure. Their process is the art of forging change in material things. This craft goes back in history thousands of years.

Fire, a component in the process of blacksmithing, is a metaphorical aspect in psychology. Its three-pronged manifestation of heat, light, and destruction is a symbol of regeneration in mankind.

Fire burns out the impurities of metals, which leaves the dross floating on top to be thrown out, leaving only the pure metal behind. Equestrian riders burn out their dross in the arena by destroying the useless parts of themselves to aid in the achievement of their success. Call upon the ancient craft of hammer and heat. Ride through the fire and create a change in yourself.

The Farrier's Fire

Use the farrier's fire, forge your skill
with burning. Call upon the ancient
craft of hammer and heat.

Leave a burning arc around the arena.
Ride by the light of fire,
a moment's flicker becomes the flame.

The tip of the flame leaves no trace
of existence, only a moment of light.

An equestrian master rides a flaming moment,
leaving all trace of self behind.

Burn your being with fire
and become this heart flicker.

T he equestrian world is filled with individuals who are masters of their craft. Saddle makers, farriers, and trainers all provide for us a mastery of skill that we do not possess. We rely on their crafts to practice ours.

Mastery of skill is more than the mere accumulation of information. It is the understanding of all the parts of a whole and the conditions they serve. It is the attainment of the proper gesture for the appropriate craft.

The farrier knows the exact moment when metal is ready to shape, the saddle maker understands the qualities of different leathers, and the trainer's words strike the right chord at the right time.

True mastery when riding a horse can be recognized by the instantaneous use of knowledge, a complete surrender to the act, and the effortless movement in the action involved. Horse and rider become one, and the result is harmony in motion.

To attain the heights of a skilled master takes years, it is the slow accumulation of knowledge and experience. The road is long and the aim high. Be patient for what must come slowly, and you could become a master.

The Master's Craft

The fit of a saddle is the skill of a master's craft.
The knife of a craftsman cuts the shape of beauty.

The lightness of hoof is the farrier's purpose.
Fire and hammer forge the arc of a hoof.

The hope of a trainer is the ribbon of victory.
Force of words will sever the mind's belief.

The apprentice bows to the master again and again.
You are the apprentice, cut open your equestrian heart.

Die with patience to the essence of the master.
Enter the arena of the great universe,
where horse and rider speak.

I t has always fascinated me how a horse rarely seems to carry negative emotions for things that a human being might. Without the slightest care in the world, they go about their days with an indifference to others that releases them from all attachment. This carefree attitude is entertaining to watch and, if observed closely, can bring about the most unusual delights.

On the other hand, as human beings, we fall victim to our emotions and end up feeling guilt or shame for experiences that never contained any negativity. We carry around negative emotions far beyond their usefulness by keeping ourselves absorbed in the memory of energy-sapping experiences. There is falseness in our emotional lives that we all struggle to understand.

Unlike humans, horses will never play emotional games. They never lie about how they feel and what their intentions are. They know that sincerity is the clearest way to communicate; it leaves the least room for misunderstanding. But don't be fooled by blunt honesty; even if it's positive in your horse's eyes, it might not be for you. Crying won't help either when your mount decides to surprise you with an attitude and a buck.

No Guilt

A fly lands on a single hair,
the touch of something there.

The hair twitches—the tail's
intention has a target.

Crying flies everywhere,
the tail feels no guilt.

A hard spur hits a rib,
the touch of something there.

The rib twitches—hooves lift
and touch the sky.

Crying riders everywhere,
the horse feels no guilt.

Part Two

The Joy

We need joy; it is vital to our existence. Without joy our lives stagnate. Joy is the exultation of your being from the personal bonds of limitation. It is a breaking free from the illusionary boundaries in our lives. Joy is the impersonal expansion into the greater realms of the heart.

Joy and pleasure are not the same; they feel closely related, but only the former can increase the level of your being. Pleasure is relative and is caused by the excitement of your mental states and the physical body; therefore, it is not associated with an expansion of the heart. Only the heart generates joy.

Complacency in life finds no reason to overcome an obstacle. The absence of struggle and loss keeps joy at a distance. Struggle and sacrifice, then, are the generators of joy. The more we become aware of our present state, accept our equine struggles, and learn from our experiences, the more joy we will create.

I asked the saddle blanket, "Why do you look so concerned? Why do you ask to be placed on my horse's back?"

The saddle blanket replied, "The seamstress plucked my soft white eyes from the fields of cotton, where I watched over the earth, and sewed me into this form. Now I joyfully bear the weight of a rider to watch over this horse and keep concern at bay."

As I walked into the barn down the aisle and entered the tack room, I recalled that the riders were away at a show. It was eerily quiet; there was a silence there that I had not felt before. Astonished, I noticed all the tack was gone. No bridles on the wall, no saddles on the racks. There were dusted rectangles on the floor where riders' trunks once rested, leaving only a trace of yesterdays past. It was as if the entire barn had been moved.

I walked to the doorway, gazed over the arena, and felt a longing to see my friends filling the room with their presence. I yearned for the sound of hooves turning up the footing and seeing the dust-filled air reflecting the lighted joy of circling riders. Immersed in the emotions of separation, I felt an ironic connection to the joy of horses.

We all experience separation from our horses to our loved ones; there is a universal longing we all share. Ironically, separation would not exist were it not for wholeness. The longing we feel is contained in the union once felt, showing us that all things are connected, that horse and rider are one.

Nothing Here

No saddles in the barn,
all the tack rooms empty.

Nothing left here,

only equine longing circling the arena.

T he eyes are the windows to the soul. You can see the emotional state of another by the look in his or her eyes. It reveals itself from within by the subtle gaze of a presence inside. Joyful or melancholy, the eyes will never lie; they faithfully display the state of our inner being.

A look is worth a thousand words; without the slightest sound, an expression can say it all. From the confused look of a lost foal to a longing gaze from the stall cage, the eyes express what words cannot, the constant longing for another.

Longing is a fundamental state of being alive. From the moment we're born, we persistently search to obtain a sense of communion. We long for the impersonal sense of union that comes from being deeply connected to another.

Connect to your inner being; untether yourself from seperation. Let your longing escape into the freedom of the one who wishes union—your horse, the equine soul.

The Hitching Post

No time to sit idle in the saddle,
escape your prison stall cage.

A longing gaze sifts through
barn doors dissolving into freedom.

Untie the Gordian knot from the hitching post,
release the equine soul from the one who wishes union.

W hen we fall ill to some disease, instinctively we feel the need to rest and recover. We intentionally take time away from our daily lives and seek shelter in the comfort of our homes. After a while, though, we feel a longing for friends and family. We yearn to feel the rhythm of our lives back to normal, giving us the fulfillment we need.

The experience of riding a horse after a long pause due to injury can be exhilarating. Sitting in the saddle leads to a feeling of closeness and sends the senses whirling. That cheerfulness is like a song that lifts the spirit and fills a heart with joy.

A Sound Horse

A lame horse hears silence in a lonely stall.
Standing hooves create no rhythm.

A sound horse strikes the right chord,
music to the ears of another.

Care and conversation bring a concert to the arena,
sending all a sound equine joy.

T he heart is an extraordinary organ. It unflinchingly keeps the entire body in balance and will automatically correct any injury to itself without stopping the vital work it does to keep the body functioning. More than that, the heart is the center of simplicity and the creator of peace.

Paradoxically, simplicity of the heart is found in silence, not in the intellectual contemplation of the world. Silence is the source from which all sound rises. It is the place where we find an expansion of ourselves into another, giving way to feelings of closeness and peace.

The hoof, like the heart, creates a rhythm of sound that stirs the soul and fills the mind with wonder. I enjoy listening to the sound of hooves as a horse runs across an open pasture. That rhythmic sound creates in me feelings of courage and strength of which the origins are unknown. I find myself focusing on my heart and feeling the freedom of simple thoughts that are devoid of intellectual complexity and contradictory emotions.

Listen to the sound of thunder; hear the beat of an equestrian heart. Expand your soul into another. Ride the sound of silence, where horse and rider find a home.

Thunder Rises

Thunder rises from the dust of hooves.
That sound—a heart.

Listen to the heart,
the silence of thunder's home.

That is where you should ride,
even though you sit in the saddle.

W henever I ride a horse through nature, the first thing I realize is the overwhelming sense of peace. Riding down a trail, I begin to experience my senses lowering their attachment to the outside world yet becoming more attuned to every sound and sensation. I notice my horse releasing tension as its walk becomes relaxed, slow, and smooth. My saddle fits in a way I don't often feel as it accepts my weight in perfect balance, giving me constant awareness of my horse's state. I drop my reins and let my horse lead the way. Without effort, I feel a deep harmony with my horse and the surroundings.

As I lower the excitement of my three functional states of being—the intellectual, the emotional, and the physical—I find myself entering into silence. Saddle, bridle, and reins work in absolute unison as we walk together down the trail in a flaming moment of complete silence.

Silence is a place where the immobility of thought begins to open the inner ear near the central region of our chest, the heart. Silence is where we discover the place in our hearts that we call home.

The Spark of Silence

A saddle appreciates the weight of a rider.
It yearns to receive the worn colored look of its use.

Many nights...eyes stare from a stall
into the tack room longing for the touch of leather.

A bridle accepts the taste of hay on steel.
Sometimes reins turn of their own accord.

Nature knows that home is where the heart lives.
These things fall into silence where they belong.

Ride your heart where the
spark of silence feeds the flame.

I often hear inexperienced riders say they have a fear of falling. It's a long way down from the lofty back of a horse. Yet the courage they show in the saddle is astounding. But courage comes in more than physical form; it also has a psychological aspect to it. The courage of the heart is something else altogether.

The fear of letting go and experiencing the unknown puts you face to face in a state of silence with your own insecurities. But don't be afraid; the silent well we fall into has at the bottom a treasure.

When we empty the mind of its useless chatter, we begin to experience silence. We find ourselves in a state of emptiness like that of a vacuum waiting to be filled. So what fills this space that has been emptied? What rises from a bed of silence? Paradoxically, it is the heart.

In silence of the heart, treasures rise to the surface, and, without our effort, intuitive knowledge saturates our being, giving way to the wealth of wisdom. However, the mind is tenacious, and thoughts will soon appear. The automatic train of routine thoughts and emotions will keep you on the bottom of the well with nothing to show for falling.

Don't be afraid of falling from your horse; find the quickest way to the bottom, and fall into another's heart.

Silken Thread

It can be a new day, but the same old way.
Reach for the now and it will present itself.

The moon always shows you the same view,
but stare long enough and it will drop its sullen face.

Remember when falling not to be scared,
you could land in the well of wisdom.

Gaze up from the place you fell into,
and you can see the light.

The quickest way to fall is into another's heart.
Your horse has a heart bigger than your own.

Fall where the great equestrian heart dwells,
rest on a golden saddle blanket.

Then your riding will change, and you will find
something more than wealth or prestige.

You will find the silken golden thread
that makes two hearts one.

C ommunication takes many forms; it can be spoken, written, or given an entirely different platform like music. Each form gives the same expression different meanings, allowing subtleties in communication that are virtually endless.

As you read the poems in this book, you may not realize that the information I convey is not contained in the words. Words don't contain information; they transmit it. We understand one another through the agreed-upon symbolical meaning that each letter and word represents. Those symbols placed in the correct order create a language. We use language to communicate.

Whenever I'm in an environment where people and horses are interacting, there is always communication taking place. From horse to horse or person to person, messages are sent through the language they understand. Whether it's fanciful and filled with imagination or direct and concrete, there is always something being said.

There is another form of communication; however, it speaks a different language. Most would agree that it exists, but none of us can say where. Its nature is miraculous, and its expression is beauty in all forms. It is the language of love.

We Have a Secret

We have a secret,
that which cannot be spoken.

Reins cradle the nape of the neck.
Manes flow in the wind,
beauty all around.

You give what I ask and make a salve
that heals my loneliness.
Everything I long for, you suffer remedies.

Grain settles the stomach.

Let me rest in you,
closer than my thoughts of you.

When others see the truth,
they cannot speak what cannot be spoken.

W hen we communicate with another, we need to speak from a common place of understanding. I cannot have a discourse with someone who speaks Portuguese unless I know the language. At the same time, however, we can ascertain to a certain degree the intentions of another even if we don't know the language. We can do this by relying on the flow of information through similar states.

To communicate with another being is to identify and experience the same state in which it lives. Emotion identifies with emotion and thought with thought. We've all heard the expressions between lovers that "we finish each other's sentences," or "I knew how he felt."

The language of the heart is the state of our inner being; its essence rests in the wisdom of expansion. The language of the mind is of the outer world; its use is that of dissection, and its result is separation. The mind and the heart find it difficult to communicate because they speak from uncommon states.

Speak to your horse on common ground, that of the heart. Leave the world and your desires behind; ride unrestricted to a new understanding of the heart.

Where Reins Break New Ground

There is knowledge beyond knowing.
It rests here on my horse's back,
in his heart.

Information fills me with time and space,
but he knows it has no dimension.

The pearl of wisdom rests inside the
common breath of a subtle canter.

Effort and desire mean nothing here,
where lost reins break new ground.

Horses are living miracles. They are born as all animals are with a knowledge that is inherent to their kind. They can make determinations like when they know not to eat certain plants because they are poisonous. That knowledge comes from inside its being, not from the outside world. It is beyond the world of facts. Some might call it nature like when the newborn foal instinctively knows to drink its mother's milk. This information requires no explanation to the recipient. It already exists, waiting to be used.

All living things contain inherent knowledge. A kernel of grain is no different. On the outside is a shell, the hard, fibrous casing that protects the vital center. Inside are all the nutrients required for growth with the knowledge to know when to sprout.

This information is different from the knowledge you learn. You can learn all the points of a horse, but that doesn't tell you anything about the animal. To gain a true understanding, you must look at the horse, which relationships it has, and how it acts. That will tell you more about a horse than any name ever could.

The Heart of the Matter

There is a kernel of golden grain
in the chest of your horse.

Slip inside the golden grain,
become the kernel of knowing.

Ride the heart of the matter,
not the ground beneath.

In the equestrian world, there has always been a lot of talk about technique. Every trainer and rider has his or her own techniques, each based on knowledge and experience, every one being valuable. Technique in the dressage arena is one kind, in the jumper ring another, and in the western world yet another. Despite the varying disciplines, they all share the same desire of order and control while in the saddle.

Nature has its own technique. It stems from the inner world, not the outer. A horse's ears will twitch at the sound of a hay wagon, and its tail will sway to keep flies away in the summer. It gives order to whatever form it resides in; it has a discipline all its own. These functions are automatic, and they happen without thought or consideration.

Once we learn a technique to perfection, it also becomes automatic. There is little thought in the execution of a balanced canter. It ends up like the technique of nature, serving a purpose with order and control. Leave behind the exterior world, and ride the rhythm of a heart.

Leave Behind

Ears twitch from the sounds of the hay wagon,
that movement knows nothing of technique.

The stomach neighs in anticipation of a meal.
Hay is turned to manure without effort.

Riding a horse is more than technique,
the trainer's words are only suggestions.

Who gives the heart its beat?
Death is real, but only to the body.

Leave behind the thinker's thoughts,
sit in the axis of the chest.

Feel the beat of the great equestrian heart
that moves to the rhythm of its own technique.

W e all realize the importance of feeding our horses the proper nutrition. Fresh hay and clean water aid in the support of a healthy body. Frequent time away from the stall and socializing with other horses create a balanced spirit. Proper grooming and constant care add to the overall quality of your horse's life.

Just like humans, horses have individual needs and desires. Some of us like the attention of crowds, and others prefer their solitude. One thing is for sure, though; we all enjoy the company of someone who gives his or her undivided attention to us. The feeling of being watched by a parent or held by a friend provides for us a deeper sense of love and security than might be achieved by a minimum of care.

Give your horse something more. Kind words and a soft touch go a long way toward building a relationship with your horse.

Sweet Talk

You can feed your horse,
hay nourishes the body.

Any animal needs the earth,
but that is not all.

Feed the soul and it will respond,
sweet talk and loving hands
nourish far more than the body.

There are two forms of thankfulness. One is the outward acknowledgment of a gift received or an expression being offered. The other is the inner recognition of a perception between reality and illusion. Both forms serve a valuable purpose in our lives.

There are also two forms of knowledge, inner and outer. Outer knowledge is relative in that it depends on the acuteness of the perception and the association of its place in our minds. Inner knowledge is a state of assimilation with the state or being of another. It is the direct cognition of inner intuitive experiences that expand your being, resulting in joy.

Horses, like humans, have an inner knowledge available to them. This is the innate knowledge of nature that in myriad ways shows itself constantly. We all can sense danger. Horses will instantly know the state of another in the herd or the intent of a predator nearby. Different from that, though, it will have to learn where the hay is thrown every night at feeding time.

Increase the thankfulness in all areas of your life. Be thankful for the expansion of joy from the union of knowledge in the movement of horse and human. It will resound in you the depths of your own presence and radiate your joy to the heart of another!

My Horse

My horse, my heart...
You give your soul for my pleasure,
taking only from me what you need.

I apologize for asking you to do what
I know you don't understand.

I ask you to jump but tell you to turn.
Yet you clear the heights anyway.

I ask for six strides and you give seven,
because you knew that was right.
I wish I could say the same.

I live between the guilt, because I'm
stuck there asking for forgiveness.

You live now for yourself in the joy
of your own movement. I can see the
difference but still don't know how.

My horse, my heart...
Fill me with your radiance so I might
know for a moment the presence in your eyes.

I often hear people commenting on the things that they don't have. If I only had a nicer car or a bigger house then I would be happy. We all fall at times under the illusion that materialism will bring us happiness. Make no mistake about it: a nice home will bring you comfort, and a quality car will give you reliable transportation. But these things are ephemeral, and we cannot rely on them for any deeper sense of joy. For that, we must focus on the heart.

When I was a child, my family had horses. They lived in our backyard in a small, fenced paddock. I had a fondness for one in particular; he was an aging black and white we named Silver. He didn't have the sought-after pedigree that others typically desire, but to me it didn't matter. I remember people commenting on his weathered look and unsightly conformation. He was in the later years of his equestrian life and had acquired a nagging limp from an old knee injury. He was kindhearted and always showed a willingness to please.

I liked Silver because others didn't; there was a proud grit in the way he kept on despite his aging condition. When I rode him around our property, he would limp, and I would giggle as the injury added an extra motion to his walk that I found amusing. I think he sensed that I enjoyed his disabilities, and he gave to me something in return—his heart. He taught me to ride the heart, not the pedigree.

No Pedigree

The beauty of a ride is not in the bloodline.
The strength of a rider doesn't fall on titles,
it falls on courage.

The master trainer can give away his words.
You can purchase a lesson but not know how to ride.

Fear springs from the sound of comparison.
That is the outside. Go inside for what you desire.

Say yes to the heart of the matter. Ride the heart.
Inside of that, there is no pedigree.

W henever I'm at a barn, I notice that the atmosphere is light and filled with joy. The conversation is filled with laughter and stories about horses. The people there are doing what they love and are living in the moment.

The elusive present—here one instant, gone the next. It takes discipline to keep our minds in the now. It's something that eludes us for our entire lives. We unconsciously remember the past and use it as a guide to the present, not realizing that today is new and yesterday's gone.

Horses seem to live in the present more than we do. They can be stressed about their immediate environment but generally not some future event. They naturally follow the immediate need of the present in a way that we will not. We let our minds wander into the imaginative world, which is not part of the present environment. Quite often it creates difficulty where none really exists. It can cause us to experience fear when none is there or give us false hope about an upcoming event.

Leave your fears behind; learn to ride the disciplined moment. Grow from the only place you can, inside the delight of now.

Learning to Ride

Don't let your training become distracted.
Don't watch dust rise from the bouncing
tails of other horses.

You will not find the present there.
It rests in a note, in the drumbeat
sound of a hoof.

Learning comes from the sound of joy,
not from the dusty images of yesterday.

A horse will lead itself to water.
You can lead yourself to the now.

There...training has no purpose,
where learning rides itself.

So often in life we focus on what we want rather than what we have. This preoccupation gives rise to anxiety in the present with impatience about the future and sets forth in us a struggle that has little value. Why would you give up the joys of today for the hope of tomorrow?

Success is found in the moment, not from the fleeting hope of tomorrow's delight. Work from a place of joy, and all the rest will fall into place. Your efforts will be rewarded due to your concentration and growth, not from denying your happiness until your goals are reached. Don't find yourself at the end of an empty dream, facing the truth that you sacrificed years of happiness for a moment's delight.

Never train with an eye on the future while forgetting about today. There is more to hard work and dedication than grave seriousness. Become a true champion, and find success along the way.

The Color of Gold

Results from training hide in the color of gold,
the winner's ribbon on the barn door.

The tracks of a champion fade from sight
as the morning mist covers the arena.

The equine ego turns about a center,
the life of a horse beats in the center of the chest.

Everything rests inside the outside,
a world in a world.

Standing in the winner's circle lasts a moment,
the time to get there—years.

Never train looking for gold,
ride instead all the colors of the rainbow.

G enerosity is a quality we all can aspire to have. Human generosity is the ability to surrender your sense of self in the service of another. When we give, however, it is generally a mixture of our hope to provide for another and a secret sense of personal benefit. When we receive, we can experience a burden that requires an action to settle an imbalance. Only an altruistic act without compensation can result in a higher sense of giving.

Equine generosity follows its own sense of altruism. A mare will protect its foal from harm even if the result is her own death, serving the greater good of the herd. She will nurse and care for an orphan without pity or regret. These acts of generosity are circular states binding themselves together through the undying quality of natural harmony.

Every circle returns to itself, but the end result is the state in which it began, either returning to the mind, with all its complexities, or to the heart, which whispers a union all its own.

Sweeping Whispers

Out of your generosity
an endless arc is formed.

The curve of a hoof,
the track of a tail.

Great sweeping whispers
gather on your breath,
circling round the universe.

One tangent finds a home,
whispering to my heart.

I was at the local barn one Sunday afternoon watching everyone going about the business of riding their horses. I overheard two adults having a conversation about the latest techniques of horsemanship. One said, "You have to remain in control of your horse; only strict discipline will get results." The other one replied, "I think self-control is the key to making your horse respond." As I listened to them banter back and forth with the seriousness of a judge, I saw a young girl riding her horse around the arena going completely unnoticed. She was in a rhythmic canter that seemed effortless as if she could ride forever. There was a smile on her face, and her pony seemed to enjoy the experience as much as she did. It was a thing of beauty, watching the two of them share such a wonderful experience. I smiled as I realized that the child knew nothing of the latest theories that the others were still arguing about.

It became clear to me that results from training do not necessarily come from a strictly defined practice or theory. It also comes from the experience of joy, where each turn is alive in the geometry of union. Ride your horse with the abandon of a child; leave your technique behind, and form together turns of joy.

The Equestrian Soul

Have you ever ridden the equestrian soul?
Many people ride with their eyes open
but their hearts closed.

Ride with the awareness of a child in the saddle.
In that innocence is the communion of souls!

What is your destination? Riding little circles
around the arena? Stop exchanging hay for manure.
History is tired of the endless circle of itself.

Ride instead the great arc of the equestrian soul,
that is a circle that can't be repeated.
Its crescent is aware and fresh, alive in geometry.

Learn from a child on a pony. Every tangent is a new
turn formed from geometric joy.

We intertwine our lives with horses' because they give us something rare in this world: friendship. Whether it's a tough day from a rough ride or a long walk on a short trail, it's all the same to us—a closer friend and lasting memories.

Our friendships help to define our lives. They provide for us a sense of connection to the world. Each one holds a unique place and a different meaning in our lives. In part, friendships are formed by definitions. They create a model by which we gauge our positions in the world and to each other. The more constricting our definitions, the further apart our relationships grow, and the broader our thinking, the more connection we feel to the world.

Keep your relationships simple. Expand your definitions, and feel a greater connection to the world. Make friends with joy, and you will see your friendships multiply.

Ride the Joy

Confidence and doubt ride the same horse.
The strong and soft rein steer the same direction.

The sunset and the sunrise have different meanings.
Yet both shine from the same light.

Advanced and beginner make arguments about skill.
The child rides to make friends with joy.

Improve your friendship, not your skill.

T ypically, it is difficult to find a feeling of wholeness in our lives. We struggle from day to day, attempting to join our separate existences. We rarely see life as something other than parts of a whole. We usually experience moments of complexity and separation, not union. When we finally see something from the perspective of wholeness, the opposing parts fall away, and the once-maddening confusion of conflicting ideas comes together in a burst of understanding, growing our consciousness and expanding our hearts.

It is confounding to believe that exterior forms remain separate, but interior states can join in union. This takes place inside the heart. Light and crystal never meet, but, brought together, they form a colored sky. The experience of expansion is the melting together of entirely opposing forms where the miraculous nature of unity in complexity takes place.

Heart to Heart

Love is one, all in everything.
The hoof cannot speak of the horse.
Two hearts speak of one.

Two hearts; one human and one horse,
both inside the cage of flesh.
Two of a kind, make one.

Don't deceive yourself, a diamond in the ground
or one in your pocket is still the same.
Exterior forms are nothing, only the essence remains.

Diamonds break the spectrum of light,
a rainbow's breath, inside a shimmer.
Each needs the other to make the colored sky.

Horse and human never meet.
Two hearts feel the same.

W hen horses greet each other, they often breathe into the nostril of the other. It is believed that this is a form of communication that expresses the intention of one horse toward another. It has also been said that breathing into the nostril of a horse helps to calm the animal, aiding it in trusting you. You see this today in barns and pastures across the world.

Breathing is one of the most intimate functions we perform. It is connected to the individual experience of being. The breath is a common ground from which we can experience the soul of another. It is a place of natural rhythm where separation dissolves and horse and rider become a single being in motion. I have often heard riders say, "I felt inside the breath of my horse."

Listen to the breath of your horse, and hear a trust that cannot be broken.

The Heart of a Thousand Horses

You are the heart of a thousand horses.
Where is the heart?
Where is the soul?

It rests in you,
in the communion of the breath of a gallop,
where horse and rider are one.

W e seldom feel the reality of the universe, that all things are one. We look out from the center of our lives and notice that boundaries are everywhere. We use our minds to argue differences and then point out the separation we feel. We find it difficult to grasp the idea that we have a communion with all life as we spend our lives believing otherwise.

The mind holds strong to these separate ideas and rarely gives up its superior throne to the greater reality that lies beneath. It will believe that different words can have the same meanings like synonyms in a dictionary, but the experiences of union are few and far between.

There are times, though, that we get a glimpse of something greater than ourselves such as the experience of likeness between friends. Feeling tired at the end of the day, the mind begins to relax its grip on the ephemeral world, differences fall away, and horse and rider blend together into one.

Synonyms

End of the day, covered in clay from the arena.
I'm too tired for separation.

Bitter conversations turn to majesty.
The arena has no walls.

Exhaustion like surrender brings my friend near,
horse and human synonyms.

L ife is a struggle; it is the constant effort to break down the obstacles in ourselves to attain something unique. It is the effort to increase your discomfort. Whatever your position in life, if you want to increase your abilities, it must be done with effort. The higher your achievements, the more effort it takes to get there. This is especially true when it comes to changing yourself, like a shift in your character or an improvement in skill.

During the process of change, there is the inevitable fluctuation of energy available to complete your goal. When you start out, energy is in abundance, and you are given a false sense of effort to accomplish your task. As the process moves ahead, the realization of the enormity of your ideas starts to sink in. Energy becomes decreasingly easy to come by, and the smallest effort requires strength. There can be a sense of wandering and a loss of order as you regain the concentration to continue. When the goal is seen, your false impression that the end is near reduces your efforts to finish the task. But, to the contrary, your efforts must be increased as you push through the final phase to accomplishment.

The process of change is an enormous undertaking. In order to attain something unique, increase your effort, until it becomes a joy.

Comfort

Character is born from the struggle to produce something unique.

Like a mare giving birth to the new foal.

Marc Ness was born in Billings, Montana, and received his education from Montana State University, where he earned a bachelor's degree of science in psychology. He has a personal interest in mysticism and poetry. He has an affinity for horses, and enjoys the outdoors. He lives in Superior, Colorado.

www.ingramcontent.com/pod-product-compliance
Lightning Source LLC
Chambersburg PA
CBHW031341040426
42443CB00006B/424